FRESH STARTUP

8 BUSINESSES FELONS CAN START RIGHT OUT OF PRISON

By

MICHAEL LEWISTON

Copyright © 2018 by Michael Lewiston

All rights reserved. No part of this publication may be reproduced, distributed, or transmitted in any form or by any means, including photocopying, recording, or other electronic or mechanical methods, without the prior written permission of the publisher, except in the case of brief quotations embodied in critical reviews and certain other noncommercial uses permitted by copyright law. For permission requests, write to the publisher, addressed "Attention: Permissions Coordinator," at the address below.

Cantonfield Media
2367 Tacoma Aveenue South
Tacoma, WA 98402
253-353-2011
www.cantonfield.com

Ordering Information:
Quantity sales. Special discounts are available on quantity purchases by corporations, associations, and others. For details, contact the publisher at the address above.

Printed in the United States of America
First Printing, 2018
ISBN: 978-1986068833

DEDICATION

To My Wife,
For always having my back and encouraging
me to follow my dreams.

MORE TITLES FROM MICHAEL LEWISTON

Clean Slate: 9 Secrets to Getting a Job, Even With a Felony

Your Ultimate Year of Success: 365 Secret Ways To Be A Better Leader, Get Ahead in Business, and Conquer Your World

TABLE OF CONTENTS

Introduction	1
1. Writer	15
2. Publisher	29
3. Editor	43
4. Graphic Designer	55
5. Photographer	71
6. Building Websites	85
7. Computer Programmer	101
8. Chef	115
Conclusion	127

INTRODUCTION

If you're an ex-offender who has recently been released from prison or jail, finding and sustaining gainful employment can be one of the hardest things you can do. When you walk into that interview and the employer sees that you're an ex-offender, they look at you in a way that makes your blood boil. You may feel like you want to yell at them, shake them, and make them see you for who you actually are, and not for the mistakes you made in your past. Course, you'd catch another case if you did that.

No matter how much you've changed or how

much you've cleaned up for the better, seems like some people just aren't willing to take a chance on someone who's made mistakes. They will only see you as a person who broke the law and imagine you'll be back in prison soon or hurt their business somehow.

In my book, Clean Slate, I laid out nine secrets every ex-offender can use to increase his or her chances of getting a steady job. They range from tried and true techniques, to modern ways to use email and the internet, to reach out and find those rare, convict-accepting jobs.

But I also recognize that sometimes no matter how many secrets you use, you'll never get some people to change their minds about you. The deck is stacked against you and you need another card to play.

That's why I wrote this book.

If you can't find an employer to take you on, to give you a chance to proving yourself worthy of helping their business grow and prosper, then you should take a chance on yourself. It's never been easier these days to start your own business and begin making money right away, and for some felons, this may be the only option.

If your conviction has prevented you from finding employment, even if it's been a while since you worked, starting your own business and running a company of your own is a worthwhile goal. Even if you have found a job, the type of folks who hire people with felonies are not always good to work for and you might be looking for something different. That's what I found, at least.

When I first got out, I was lucky and blessed to find a job with a home-improvement company. I worked in their marketing department because I was good with words and had a head for getting folks to sign up for a visit from the sales staff. I quickly found out, however, that the owner of the company treated everyone badly, even the customers, and routinely lied about the quality of the product. He even shorted me on my paycheck and when I mentioned it, he laughed and asked what I was going to do about it. It was a bad situation.

I needed a new job but quickly found out how hard it was to find a job as a felon. Company after company told me that hiring me was just too risky. The few companies I did work for, the ones eager to hire someone in a bad situation with a checkered past, treated me badly and were not the kinds of businesses you want to work with for any length of time. I realized something else was needed.

So, while working for a company that only hired me because they could pay me less than everyone else (knowing I was hard up for work), I learned how to build websites and market online. Because online marketing has a lot to do with writing, I also learned how to write well and began writing books and marketing those as well.

Between income from books, consulting for local businesses, and marketing/web design work, I was able to quit the job that didn't appreciate my talents and started working for myself.

Starting my own business and working for myself proved to be more rewarding and also more frustrating than I had thought possible. When I sat down to get a new client, they never ask me about my criminal background, only how I could help their business make money. My clients didn't care about my mistakes in the past, never even had one bring it up. They just wanted to see my portfolio of work. Granted, that portfolio was light in the beginning but as I did more work and kept on practicing, it grew along with my client base. I also made more products which sold passively online. But it was not all roses and champagne. While it was nice to be judged on my talent, and not on my past, being the boss was crazy hard.

I found out that running a business – or several businesses in this case – meant you had to wear all the different hats. You had to be good at getting new clients, and then you have to worry about keeping them. You have to know how to spend your money wisely, keep track of every cent, then save at least a third for taxes. Taxes are a whole chapter by themselves and as a small business owner you have to know about them or you will run into more trouble than you want. If you didn't catch a case with the Feds, let me tell you that it's not a pleasant experience. If you have employees you have to think about managing, scheduling, payroll, benefits, and the culture of your workplace. But there are plenty of books about these things. First things first; you have to know what you want to do.

I've come up with a list of eight businesses you can start, most with little to no money required in the beginning. There are hundreds more you could start, but this list should cover most people and shows you what is possible if you decide to pursue self-employment. It's not an easy road but it's so rewarding when you finally make the decision to take the plunge.

You don't have to pick just one of these business ideas either. You can choose between them all at different times to make a living. Or combine them into interesting hybrids; for instance, you can give tours, take video or pictures of the excursion, and offer those services at an addition fee. Or have an Etsy store for your pottery and painting, run a blog for other store owners, and sell a course teaching people all the things you have learned while setting up your own store. The best thing is you can keep updating your offerings because you never stop learning!

When you work for someone else, you are trading time for money. You give your limited time, the one truly non-renewable resource, for a wad of cash, and then have to trade more time for more cash. This is the world most people live in and it's often insulting how little cash we get for our precious time. To make matters worse, when you have a felony, a large percentage of employers don't even want to give you money for your time. It's an insult to your injured career and life.

Thankfully, you don't have to take it. You can be the boss now and start living a life full of possibility and success despite, and maybe because of, your incarceration.

You don't have to read about every job I recommend, you can skim to see what looks interesting and then read more in-depth on the topic. Some topics have more information than others because higher startup costs mean those businesses are more complicated to run. In fact, it often adds to the complication because you can't pay people to do things for you.

One example of this is becoming a publishing author. You would have the ability to write, create, and publish your own books, but writing is only one part of that particular profession. You have to know how to weave a good narrative and format your writing, so it can be published. You'll need to design book covers, upload and market your books, and much more. You can always pay other people to do these tasks—even the writing if you want—but if you don't have the money to do so you'll end up having to do all of the work yourself, which means you'll need to learn how to accomplish all of those tasks.

Learn how to be your own boss, take control of your destiny, start making money, and create your own future. Pick one or more of these jobs and get one your way!

FRESH STARTUP

1.
WRITER

WRITER DESCRIPTION

You can write anywhere these days and good writers will always be in demand because there is always something to be written. With the wealth of writing opportunities out there, including articles, promotional content, academic writing, blog posts, etc., many companies and even individuals look at content as the new face of marketing. It is the fastest-growing way to reach out to readers and consumers, so new jobs are created every day, resulting in the need for more and more talented writers. If you can craft a good sentence and make an idea seem appealing, you can be a content writer.

Every form of writing has a different approach; content writing for a blog will differ tremendously from a piece of academic writing in terms of tone, length, subject matter, and word choice. It's important to research jobs carefully before deciding to take them on. You don't want to accept a job and then realize it will take so long to research the topic that the price is no longer worth it!

If you decide to pursue content writing, be aware that often you will not have your name attached to your work. That said, there are many reputable online agencies dedicated to connecting writers with those who need their services.

Some of the necessary skills include having a vast vocabulary and excellent knowledge of grammar, spelling, and syntax—as well as a sense of creativity. Content writers find they often they have orders to write on a wide variety of topics, including promotional blog posts for a business, ghostwriting eBooks, providing keyword-rich content for blogs and websites, etc. Choosing to write paid content is a varied and interesting job that can be lucrative and fun for those who possess the right skills.

WRITER COST

The cost of writing is almost next to zero. All you need is a paper and a pen, and you are good to go. However, to grow your business, you will eventually need a personal computer, as this makes it much easier to check for spelling and grammar mistakes. An internet connection is also very important. Using the internet makes it possible not only to link up with clients, but also to do the necessary research for whatever article or content you happen to be working on. Also, the majority of clients nowadays prefer work to be submitted in a digital format, and many now prefer to make payments electronically, as well.

The biggest upfront cost is time: time to research, to connect to clients, to build a portfolio, and to hone your writing talents to a professional level. Any freelance work requires time and patience to get to a point where you can make a livable wage.

WRITER DIFFICULTY

Writing can be easy or difficult depending on the niche. Academic writing would require an extensive knowledge of the subject matter before you can write anything. Content writing and articles are less tricky to write and would require you to either write with a more conversational tone or give your opinion on the topic at hand. Most articles will require at least a little research, though. It's important to at least be able to give the impression that you know what you are talking about. Many clients will also want you to show some sources and possibly add links to web content, so some degree of formatting will be required.

Writing can be time-consuming if you have a shallow knowledge of the subject. There is also the possibility that your client may reject your work, prompting you to redo it. The basic skill needed for writing is attention to detail, coupled with a working knowledge of whichever language you write in. This alone will save you a whole lot of troubles, as those who are able to self-edit (and do it well), not only have a higher chance of their work being accepted, but also a much higher rate of repeat clients. And it's a well-known fact that it's the repeat clients who form the backbone of any business.

An added bonus of working with the same people is that as you get to know what they are looking for and write several articles or blog posts on the same topic, you gain a better understanding of it. This makes it so that you don't have to do as much research and are able to write at a greater speed, with more confidence and ease. The pay stays the same, but you work a whole lot less.

STARTING A WRITING BUSINESS

To start this business, all you need to do is to look for clients who need something written and propose to do the work for them. There are also online marketplaces from which clients may be sourced, without anyone asking if you are an ex-convict.

Be aware that many clients will ask you to provide a portfolio, or writing samples, before they hire you. Some will ask for samples related to the job itself, while others want more general writing, in order to get a feel for your style and see if it is a good fit for their needs.

In any case, it is wise to build up a portfolio of your writing—several pieces in different styles and tones, and a variety of word-lengths and topics. For example, you will want to show that you can write in an authoritative, corporate style, but also that you can produce a piece that is more casual. The key to making money from content writing is being able to wear a lot of hats, whether you are producing stuffy-sounding copy for the newsletter of a bank or writing a fun article about training dogs. Show your skills, prove that you can do the job, and keep at it. Freelance writing is difficult to get going, but once you have some regular clients, it can be amazingly well-paid and even fun.

2.
PUBLISHER

PUBLISHER DESCRIPTION

If you can't write, maybe you know people who can. Lots of guys in your block or wing might be writers and would love the opportunity to get published. Publishing has to do with packaging a book for sale. It can be traditional (the print-on-paper type of publishing), or it can be electronic (eBooks and the like).

Traditional publishing is a difficult business to break into, as it requires a lot of start-up capital. Electronic publishing is ridiculously easy, and as more and more people start to read exclusively using Kindles or Nooks, the market is only going to get bigger.

As a publisher, it is your job to offer promotion, formatting, editing and a flashy cover to your writers. They look to you to sell their books, but this can only happen if you do your research and learn how the industry works. Nowadays, with electronic publishing especially, the market changes so frequently it can be a full-time job just to keep up! Bestselling genres change from day-to-day, as do trends within genres. It's important, as a publisher, not only to know how to create a finely-crafted book that anyone would love to read, but also to know your audience.

This job requires attention to reviews, interaction on social media, and carefully studying the buying/selling trends of your targeted audience.

PUBLISHER COST

The cost of publication will depend on the type of publication you intend going into. Ink-on-paper publication can be very expensive because it would require you to have certain heavy machines for the following operations: binding, filming, stripping, typesetting, pages, mechanicals, etc. These could cost you thousands of dollars, so this may not be a good idea just yet. Electronic publication is at absolutely zero cost. All you need to do is create an account with an online vendor, format the book properly and upload it. It automatically becomes available to anyone across the world. Some of the popular online book vendors are; Amazon, Barnes & Noble, Kobo, Smashwords, Google Play, etc.

PUBLISHER DIFFICULTY

Publishing requires dedication and time. Just as books are not written in a day, editing them and formatting them for public consumption is a very time-consuming occupation. Occasionally, a book will need several revisions before it is ready to be released. Making sure that your final product is the very best it can be is the most important part of being a publisher. With that in mind, it's important to be discriminating in what you publish. If you wouldn't want to read something, why do you think anyone else would? Choose a genre or two that you are really passionate about, build your reputation as a reliable publisher in that genre, and you will soon have your pick of well-written books by authors clamoring to work with you.

Another important part of publishing is creating awareness of your published work. Promotion of the books you publish can be costly and time-consuming, but if no one even knows it exists, how can they buy it? What is the use of a publication if it never gets to be read? You need to build your reputation on social media because that is the easiest place to get an audience. Share pre-publication teasers, set up giveaways, constantly update on your latest products. Share the links to your publications on your social media platform and encourage feedback.

Actually, listen to the feedback. When your audience is telling you exactly what works and what doesn't, or what they want to see more of, what they're tired of, it becomes much easier to produce books that they are likely to buy, read and recommend to others.

STARTING A PUBLISHING BUSINESS

To start a publishing business, you will need a good editor and a graphic artist to design the book covers. A great book cover is the key to selling your books. With millions of books out there, you will need a captivating cover to catch the attention of stray readers. It's possible to design book covers yourself, as well. All you need is photo-editing software, an eye for design and color, and access to stock photos or images in the creative commons. Learning to create beautiful or interesting covers that will garner attention is easy, but as with any skill, requires patience and practice. You may go through dozens of designs before you find one that satisfies both you and your writer. Keep at it, look at the covers of bestselling books in the genre you're targeting, see what they're doing to get attention and try for the same. Being able to create your own book covers is a skill that will save a lot of money in the long run, as many designers charge upwards of $100, especially if they are well-known.

An editor is important because even if people buy your books, once they encounter spelling or grammar errors in the content, or sense a lack of continuity, they will likely stop reading (no matter how good the story is) and never pick up another of your books. Worse, they will likely mention it in any reviews, hurting your chances of further sales. A good editor can be expensive, but it's one of those costs that are just necessary. Unless you're a professional editor or proofreader, this is not something you can do yourself. If you have a great story with a great cover, why risk the chance of it being a dud because of some errors? Pay for an editor and get a good one.

As your reputation as a publisher grows, your audience will eventually grow along with it. However, that will only happen if you do not undermine the quality of your publications. Give your readers a good product and they will always come back for more.

3.
EDITOR

EDITOR DESCRIPTION

Editing is a necessary step when it comes to producing a wonderful story or article. Think about it: if you can't read something because it has a lot of flaws, whether they are grammatical or in spelling or continuity, how do you expect others to want to read it? This is the idea that keeps editors – especially good ones – in business! Most people know that Spellcheck is incapable of catching every flaw, so a pair of real eyes is needed.

An editor needs to work closely with the author to spot flaws in the plot, sentence construction, spelling, and grammar. For this reason, it is also necessary to understand how a good story comes together. Editors will often suggest small plot details to make the entire manuscript come to life or suggest that parts be moved around to improve the flow of the story. Editing is not just about catching misspelled words and poorly-placed punctuation. Editors are often the ones who make a piece of writing resonate with readers.

The reason for this is that a writer often finds it difficult to spot their own flaws. The human brain, while a magnificent piece of machinery, will often see what it expects to see. Whether it's a word that is spelled differently or an entire missing sentence that gives a later passage sense, more than one set of eyes on a piece of writing is invaluable.

A writer needs a fresh pair of eyes, and a good editor will not just point out what doesn't work but will give the author feedback on how to make it work. Creating a good piece of writing is a collaborative effort, with all the necessary pieces falling into line due to the combined work of a select few.

EDITOR COST

You cannot talk of being a good editor if you do not have an excellent command of the English language. While you may speak and write very well, as well as read extensively and know how a good story is created, there are many parts to this complex language that require study. Striving to become a good editor may mean that you will need to get a BA or Masters in English. There is no shortcut to getting that besides going back to school. The cost here should come from the tuition fees and all other academic related costs.

If you truly cannot afford to go back to school, there are many programs online that offer training in English for free. The good part about being a freelancer is that many clients will want to see results rather than a diploma. Set up a good portfolio (this may require some free editing when you are just starting out), demonstrate flexibility and strong communication skills, and there will always be a client out there for you. Just remember, this is not a job to just jump into, it takes time and sometimes money to build the skills you will need to be a good editor.

EDITOR DIFFICULTY

In editing, the watchword is, "the slower the better." You have to take your time reading documents line by line to be sure you have mopped up all of the errors, or at least ninety-nine percent of them. Think about it, you wouldn't rush through a job if you want to do it well, or even thoroughly. Editing requires a high amount of mental dedication, paying close, thorough attention to every word you read, as well as considering it in the context of the sentence, the paragraph, and even the work as a whole. To properly edit a story or an article masterfully, you need to give it your full attention and a lot of your time.

The work becomes even more tedious if you are working with a first-time writer. Many writers who have never published or had anything edited before, will not understand the importance of the editor's role in their work. They may also not understand how time-consuming and expensive the process can be. By far, though, the biggest frustration will likely be that suggestions fall on deaf ears. Editing is very time-consuming, and you need to wear your robe of patience. If this job is for you, remember that you were hired for your skills and try to make the best suggestions you can.

The basic steps every good editor should follow are: work with your author to know exactly what they expect from you, catch the errors, and give constructive feedback. Whether your feedback and advice are taken to heart is another matter!

STARTING AN EDITING BUSINESS

Once you have the required qualifications, all you need to do is to convince someone who writes that you can do the job. You can even offer to edit a few pages of work for free, in order to showcase your editing skills.

One thing a lot of new editors find helpful is to stalk writing forums or websites. Once you find some writers whose work you enjoy, volunteer to do some light editing, or "beta-reading". It helps if you actually enjoy what you are reading, as the first few times it will be unpaid. Use this work to build up a portfolio, as well as a reputation for reliable, high-quality work. Once you have some rave reviews and samples to show off your skills, start marketing yourself to more commercial writers. Independent writers and those who self-publish electronically are usually more than willing to take a chance on an editor who is new to the field, especially if your rates are competitive and you show a willingness to communicate effectively and work with the writer to create an end product you are both happy to put your name on.

As with any freelance work, the ability to choose when and what you work on is invaluable, and once you have edited a few things and gained reviews, you will find that the freedom to pick and choose the projects you want not only keeps you happy with the work, but keeps you focused and intent on doing the best job you can.

4.
GRAPHIC DESIGNER

DESIGNER DESCRIPTION

If you have an eye for form and color, as well as an appreciation for fonts, graphic design may be the job for you. Creating visuals that draw people in and get them interested in a product or an idea is what this field is all about. Combining pictures or shapes with interesting color and font combinations is not something that everyone can do. To a certain extent, it takes both talent and a knack for understanding what appeals to the audience you are targeting.

As long as people continue to write, be it books, newspapers, magazines, etc., graphic designers will always be called upon to create eye-catching visual content. This may take the form of posters, book covers, advertisements, and the formatting of words and pictures in a way that flows naturally and keeps the reader engaged. It's a massively important part of any type of consumable content.

Graphic design is a form of visual communication that is attained by projecting ideas using images, words, colors, and graphic forms. One way that graphic design differs from fine art is that art is meant to evoke a feeling inside the artist, whereas designers attempt to engage their audience. Graphic designers are required for creating poster advertisements (including commercial website adverts), business branding, and so on.

Luckily, the worldwide web has opened a whole new world of opportunity for the graphic designers of today. Getting started in this industry takes little in the way of formal education, but a lot of dedication and talent. If words aren't your thing, perhaps visuals are!

DESIGNER COST

Starting a graphic design business as a freelancer can cost you from about $1,000 to $5,000, depending on how big you want to begin. If you already have a flair for drawing, then the only cost you will grapple with is that of obtaining a computer with a large amount of memory to handle a large number of both graphics and graphic-design software, like Adobe Photoshop and/or Corel Draw. A computer with a graphics card will also be invaluable, as it allows you to see images on the screen in a much higher resolution and at greater speeds than one without. This is especially important if you are working with video. It is a lot of money, but necessary for a highly-polished, professional-looking outcome.

If you do not already know how to use graphic design software, you may need to pay someone to teach you. However, there are also many tutorials and walk-throughs online. Once you have obtained your software, play around with it! Get familiar with the more popular tools and use them until you can reliably achieve the effects you are after.

Another important gadget you will need to acquire is a printer, especially if you are aiming to start big (though you could always do the designing yourself and print somewhere else, for a start). However, if you are working solely with digital or electronic graphics, or clients who need graphic design for websites, blogs, or electronic content, this won't be necessary. It might be good to start out with digital clients until you build up a large enough portfolio to target those who need printed materials.

DESINGER DIFFICULTY

The length of time it would take to complete a work of graphic design would depend on how good you are with the software. If you are new to using a computer in general, it can take months or even years to become competent with Photoshop or Corel Draw. It's also good to remember that some designs are more complicated or require more work than others. Of course, in this business, you should become able to judge the amount of work and time necessary prior to beginning a project. That way, you can provide accurate quotes and avoid billing issues further down the line. Accurate quotes also increase the chance of repeat clients.

Another skill you would need here is to understand the specifications of your client and their needs. If your client can't give a good idea of what they want, and you don't push them to communicate by asking a ton of questions and showing samples of what you can do, you will find a lot of revisions will be necessary. You won't always know exactly how to accomplish what your client wants but asking questions and keeping up a good relationship definitely helps.

Sometimes, you will find it necessary to educate your clients on why your design would work better for their needs. Your persuasive power here will help you to sell your designs, as well as create a visual that you are proud to put your name on. Remember, the whole reason a client hires a graphic designer is because they need something that will adequately market or set off their content.

STARTING A DESIGN BUSINESS

Once you have the desired software and a computer with a good graphics card, you can start graphic design. As with any freelance occupation, you will need to build a portfolio. One way to do this is to create great graphics that advertise your own business! Another option is to find something or someone online who you think could benefit from your services. Offer to create some new art for them at a discounted price if they allow you to use it to show your skills. Most small businesses or writers would jump at the chance.

If this isn't the approach you want, all you need to do is to place an advert to display some of your works. A good—and free!—way to advertise yourself is through social media and personal blogs. Don't be afraid to market yourself! Show off your various skills by making mock-ups of various types of design. Posters, ads, fan artwork for your favorite novel: if you enjoy the work, it will show in the quality.

Always remember to make sure you embed your logo or contact information somewhere on your works, to further advertise your services. A watermark on samples is also a good idea, as it helps keep others from trying to pass your work off as their own.

5.
PHOTOGRAPHER

PHOTOGRAPHER DESCRIPTION

As long as there are ceremonies such as weddings, birthdays, rallies, and so on, photographers will always be in demand. Photojournalists are very much in demand by media houses to make their publications more informative and colorful. The primary duty of a photographer is to freeze important moments and store them in soft or hard copies for future reference. The primary tool of every photographer is a camera, although in recent times that list is expanding to include things like computers and editing software.

When it comes to photography, people usually don't have anything more in mind besides expecting the photographer to produce stunning pictures for them to flaunt. As a photographer, this makes your job somewhat easy—especially if you are highly creative. It can also be challenging, because you will have to come up with something fresh and unique each and every time; otherwise, people may start to become bored with your photography work.

One good thing about being a photographer is that no one gives a damn about your identity or your past crimes or mistakes; rather, your clients will want results from you. When it comes to photography, your pictures should tell stories. They should either elicit memories or transport the person viewing it to a world they'll voluntarily agree to get lost in.

There can be a lot of bonuses to becoming a professional photographer, and one of these is the fact that you can interact with people from a variety of backgrounds and social classes.

PHOTOGRAPHER COST

For a beginner, the cost of turning your photography skills into a career will ultimately vary but will be largely dependent on getting yourself a good digital camera. You will need a camera with high number of megapixels and good "zoom" feature.

There are literally hundreds of different types of digital cameras from many different manufacturers out there to choose from, but a good camera can cost you anywhere between $300 and $1500. It is true that photography does not require you to have any fancy qualifications but enrolling in a photography course will definitely expose you to new techniques that will ultimately help you learn to take better photographs. On the other hand, you could also go online and download eBooks and other digital content created by professional photographers on the topic and teach yourself everything you will need in order to succeed. There are also many video tutorials on YouTube that could be very useful and informative for you to watch. If you intend to deliver your photographs in hard copies, then you will also need to get your hands on a good photo printer, too.

As I mentioned earlier, there are numerous software applications you can use to fine-tune your photographs. Raw, unedited photographs are not as appealing as those that are edited to high-definition perfection. Remember, you are in a competition with several other good photographers at all times, and in order to outwit them, you'll need to purchase and learn how to use basic photo editing software programs, such as Adobe Photoshop and Corel Draw. Like everything else in this world, these software programs cost money.

PHOTOGRAPHER DIFFICULTY

The main difficulty associated with photography is dealing with lighting. Too much light will blur the picture, while too little light will make it dark. A photographer needs to find the balance or learn how to use the power of lighting to create the best impression (you may need to employ artificial lighting, like a speed box). This is the same concept painters apply to their work to give it depth. Being a photographer will also require you to be agile and sacrifice your convenience to move from one place to another while covering events. If you are not ready to move from one location to the other at the shortest notification, then photography may never be for you. It shouldn't take more than a few weeks to learn some of the basic skills of photographing.

The most important thing in photography (which is also general to all visual art) is how imaginative you are. You have to be able to recreate worlds in a way that would make them appear fresh and appeal to the senses of anyone who spares them a glance. If your photographs cannot catch attention, they are as good as dead. The more people begin appreciating your photography work, the better your chances will be at gaining more clients and expanding your career.

STARTING A PHOTOGRAPHY BUSINESS

Once you have your camera hung around your neck, your career has begun. Find your way into any celebrity event and take some paparazzi shots of a celebrity. Several newspaper houses would be glad to buy your photographs (think of how Peter Parker in the movie Spiderman made a decent living as a freelance photographer, selling pictures of Spiderman).

You could also cover weddings or birthdays uninvited, making sure you have the pictures ready before the show is over so you can provide samples and hopefully attract someone to pay for them. Also, you could begin by telling your friends about your work and pleading with them to invite you if they have an event that needs to be photographed.

You do not need a thousand photographs to become a celebrity photographer; one good photograph can put you in the limelight. The life of Mark Reay is the compelling story of a photographer who started out as a homeless nobody but became one of the best fashion photographers in the world. Aligning with photography means that you would be your own boss. That is not all, you also get to make a decent living and give your social status and identity a lift from something negative to positive (instead of, when you work for someone else, that ex-convict identity never being erased from the way people look at you).

6.
BUILDING WEBSITES

WEB DESIGNER DESCRIPTION

It is impossible to deny that the world is quickly moving from analog to digital. The internet is now one of the preferred ways to convey almost any piece of information or perform any task. From online shopping, to holding online classes, to providing entertaining content, the opportunities for building a presence online are immense.

What do all of these previous jobs have in common? All of them need a website to be a reality. Nowadays, having a web presence is essential for any business or community looking to expand its global and local reach. With such huge demand, it's no wonder that web design and internet technology are some of the fastest-growing industries today.

Website designers plan, create, and update websites. These days, you may find that clients looking for professional, engaging websites need them for a variety of reasons. A business may need a website for sales or for sharing information about their services or products. They generally look for a clean, organized site that is easy for consumers to navigate. Often, they will provide a list of requirements and let the designer interpret them. Private individuals look for website designers to build more personal blogs or websites. They will want far more input to bring their vision into reality. Still others want websites dedicated to a certain theme or activity. All of these require some level of research to accurately gauge the needs of the client.

Because e-commerce is receiving more interest globally, website builders will likely never run out of job opportunities. This is a great field to get into now and build up your skills.

WEB DESIGNER COST

To be a website builder, you would need to study to be in tune with some of the terminologies you will constantly meet in the process. Programming languages such as JavaScript, HTML, CSS, PHP, and Bootstrap are a great place to start. You will also need to know something about graphic design, so a good vector graphics editor will be invaluable.

There is a lot of knowledge out there about website development, but it isn't necessary to learn through formal education. There are several free tutorials you can download from the internet and teach yourself how to do it, but more comprehensive methods involve low-priced tutorials. Often, the providers of the tutorials will be open to answering questions or going more in-depth on desired information if you are willing to pay for a course.

Of course, to be a website designer, you will need a computer. If this is something you want to pursue, consider investing in a good one. A computer with a high amount of RAM and a good graphics card is invaluable, as you will need those specs to truly make professional-looking, high-quality websites. You will also need some graphic editing software, like Adobe Illustrator.

Opening a website can cost between $500-$1,000, from hosting to your time involved. Imagine when you have several of such clients to build a website for: this is a business that can be highly lucrative for a talented designer.

The cool part of this is that you can do it from the comfort of your home, working to your own schedule and saving the cost of renting an office.

WEB DESINGER DIFFICULTY

Building a great website takes time. There is a lot of coding to be done, testing, and configuring images and text to be exactly where you want them to be. If your website has a lot of different pages, that equals more time. This is because each one has to be done separately. Luckily, there are a lot of programs and templates that will help you, especially when you are starting out.

To save time, consider saving blank templates of the pages you create. This way, you can reuse them in the future and change the content around to fit the needs of your next project.

Building a quality website will take practice. Learning coding and development is not something that can be done overnight, but with dedication and the continued building of your skills and strengths, this is something that gets easier with time.

Once you have started coding websites for others, you will need to keep up great communication. Clients want to feel as though their desires are taken into account, so it's your job to put them at ease and ensure they are getting exactly what they want. Satisfied customers are the best advertisement there is.

Being organized is also a handy skill. Taking the time to create to-do lists and organizing all files in a well-ordered system will help you immensely when it comes to the actual building.

The best web designers are those who know exactly what they are going to do next, as well as how to do it.

The best time to start building your first website is now. Build one for yourself, to advertise your services, and let your prospective clients see what you can do! The knowledge you will gain through the practice of building your first website will be incredibly valuable in the future.

STARTING A WEB DESIGN BUSINESS

Once you have studied up on how to build a website, and feel comfortable with your coding, you can build your own. Make it look professional and like a website anyone would be proud to call their own. It will be your best calling card. Consider creating different pages in different styles to showcase your abilities.

When you have your site up and running, the next step is to advertise your services. Advertising on social media is a great and free way to get your name out there but consider also reaching out to poorly designed or non-working websites to offer your services. Provide quotes and samples and keep up a high level of communication.

Make your clients feel special, like you can provide a service they can't get anywhere else, and they will always recommend you. Be sure to put your logo or contact info at the bottom of every page you create so prospective clients know where to find you.

7. COMPUTER PROGRAMMER

PROGRAMMER DESCRIPTION

Everyone wants convenience, and nowadays that takes the form of something they can easily carry about. With the rise of smartphones and tablets, portable devices are quickly becoming a ubiquitous means of accessing the internet and all it has to offer. That's where a computer programmer comes in.

Computer programmers turn all kinds of websites into apps that can run on phones, tablets, and laptops. Apps make navigating a website easy and saves the user from clicking boring web links. An important part of this job is making apps and portals that not only work but look good and are extremely user friendly.

Computer programmers also ensure the

software designed by engineers and developers can be run on computers. It requires a lot of time learning and comprehending various coding languages, testing out software to be sure that it works well, and trial and error.

This is not a job that can be learned overnight, and the world of computer programming is constantly changing and evolving as new techniques and technology are introduced.

It can also be a very fun and rewarding profession, and if you are good and can create an app or program that people find valuable and actually want to buy, it can be incredibly lucrative.

PROGRAMMER COST

To become a computer programmer, you will need to earn a degree (a two-year course in computer programming). A lot of people say that it's possible to gain the necessary skills through independent study or taking some online tutorials, but to become really good, you will need the formal education that comes with a degree. Your tuition fees will make up the bulk of expenses, but there are many programs and scholarships available for those who wish to study in the tech field. Do some research; you may find all the necessary cash available to you.

Another thing to consider is the cost of obtaining a computer. Again, you will want a fairly good one. It doesn't have to be the most expensive, but you want one with a lot of RAM and a good graphics card. You'll be writing, coding, and testing a lot of software, so you want machinery that can handle it. To go with a shiny new computer, you will need a fair amount of necessary software. Exactly what type of software will depend on the sort of programs you want to write, but most of the time it isn't cheap. Keep in mind that new versions of software are introduced regularly, so you may have to continuously upgrade to stay on top of everything. That being said, there are a lot of guides you can get for free online. They aren't a replacement for formal education, but they can be surprisingly helpful and are worth checking out.

Keep in mind, a large part of the cost is in

time. Learning any language isn't easy, and coding languages such as Java, Python and C++ are no exception.

PROGRAMMER DIFFICULTY

Besides the two years you would spend to get a degree, programming will require you to write lots and lots of code for a software to be born. This is very time-consuming, and you will find that large parts often have to be rewritten for some reason or another.

It doesn't end there; after the software has been produced, it will likely still have a lot of bugs on various operating systems and platforms. What might work on a Chrome browser will take extensive tweaking to get it to also run on an iPhone. The bad news is, unless you have every brand of smartphone or computer with all possible operating systems, you may never find out if your software really works until users begin to complain about them. At that point, you will need to go back and have them fixed. Needless to say, that as a programmer, your work on software never ends.

In order to create a program or app that people enjoy using and keep downloading, it's also necessary to understand the needs of your targeted audience. You need good customer relation skills, as well as patience. There will always be complaints, and because putting an app out means it goes to a very wide audience, you will likely be the one they complain to.

HOW TO START THIS BUSINESS

You don't need clients or special permits to develop new software; all you really need is a viable idea that people will find useful.

Often, the most successful apps and programs solve a problem or are entertaining. Game development is huge right now, and some of the most popular are the simplest.

The first step is recognizing a need that consumers have that isn't being met or is being met poorly. Develop software that can meet that need and then sell it online. It really is that simple. The complicated part is coming up with an idea for a new program or app that hasn't been done already. The most important question to ask yourself is whether your idea is better than anything out there now, and whether you have the skills to make it a reality.

Once you have your idea and the software is designed and beta tested, it's pretty simple to start making money from it. There are various online markets that can give you the leverage to sell your software, such as the Google Play Store and Apple Store. It's important to remember they will take a percentage of your sales, but they also offer your best chances for high visibility and increased downloads.

Alternatively, you can advertise your services and design programs for paying clients. Often, you will be paid a flat fee and it may not be as much as the royalties and increased earnings from independent programs. However, it is also a guaranteed payday and they will generally provide guidelines or ideas, so all you need is your set of skills.

8.
CHEF

CHEF DESCRIPTION

If you have a flare for food then you should think about satisfying people's hunger; after all, people will always get hungry. A chef gives people a taste of cuisines from far-away countries which naturally they may never have reached. Draw inspiration from Jeff Henderson, also known as Chef Jeff, who was also a felon but broke free from the stigma to become an award-winning chef. The business of being a chef is one that never goes out of style. It is the duty of a chefs to learn the recipes of various cuisines and, at some point, to develop their own for others to follow.

If you happen to be a good chef and a good writer, then you will be limited only by your own mind, because you can also produce good books based on your cooking guide for other cooks to follow. Who really cares who cooked a meal—they will either appreciate the chef or scorn them, depending only on whether if the food is sumptuous or unappealing.

Chef Jeff was a felon: he was arrested in 1987 by the San Diego Drug Tax Force and spent close to ten years of his life in prison for engaging in drugs. But it was while in prison that his love for food grew. He started working in the prison kitchen under the mentorship of Womack. When he got out of prison, he moved to Las Vegas to follow his passion. He became the first African-American executive chef at Bellagio and his memoir, 'Cooked', became a New York Times bestseller and went ahead to win multiple awards in cooking.

What caught my interest the most is that he achieved all of this without a formal cooking instruction. Who says you cannot replicate what he has done? All you need is a good guide and some cookbooks, and you are set to become the next big chef. Like Jeff, if you feel your food may receive some criticism no matter how good it is, especially by people who know your history, you could move to a new location where you are less well-known and start producing good food. In your new area, people will judge you by your food and not your past life.

CHEF COST

The capital expenditure involved in the business of becoming a chef has to do with purchasing your cooking utensils and the ingredients needed to prepare each particular dish. Every dish requires different ingredients. Paying the rent of a small kitchen may also be another financial challenge. However, as little as $500 or less can get you there, and the great part about being a chef is you can begin the very afternoon you step out of prison. Even if you do get a mentor that will guide you through the rudiments, you still need a cook book to broaden your knowledge, and all these will add to the cost.

Normally, no matter how good you may be in following the instructions of a cook book, there are cuisines you will need to see someone prepare before you can really crack them. This is where videos come in: either you buy those videos, or you subscribe to a channel where you will get them. Inasmuch as these limitations may exist, you can bypass them by first partnering with an already established cook.

This partnership will also allow you to build your customer base without sweating it out. To make life easier for you, and also bring down costs, you can liaise with vegetable farmers to supply fresh vegetable to your kitchen, thereby bypassing the rigors and extra cost of going through the middlemen. The bottom line is that there are ways you can bring down the cost of starting and running your chef business.

CHEF DIFFICULTY

No doubt, it will take time before you master your dishes and recipes, and the length of time will depend on how good you are with learning. As a chef, you will need to switch from one meal to another in a short time because every customer that comes into your restaurant will come with their own demand. You will also learn to work very quickly, as you don't want to keep your customers waiting for an eternity to be served or they may leave your place for good.

In the food industry, one very critical parameter is consistency in smell and taste. Some of your customers will definitely notice the slightest change in aroma and taste of their favorite dishes. This means you need to develop an uncanny sense of smell and taste, to be able to spot those subtle changes and correct them before they get to your customers. Another great challenge of being a chef is that you cannot hasten a meal to be ready before its time, and it is very difficult to juggle the preparation of two different meals at once. If you are not careful, you will mess both of them up. It also takes time to build your customer base, especially if you are a new chef. People will only come if they are convinced there is something they cannot get anywhere else.

HOW TO START THIS BUSINESS

There are two ways you can start a chef business. You could opt to open a small restaurant and place adverts to attract customers, or you could cook them and pre-package them in take-away plastics and go to offices to sell them (allowing the customers to come to you in the former or going to meet the customer in the latter case, the choice is yours to make).

If you are already knowledgeable about the process of producing a dish, the best way to build your business as a chef is to be part of a network of chefs, probably working in a big restaurant. As a team member, much of the pressure will be shared out among all the chefs, giving you some room to enjoy what you do while you learn. That is where you will improve your skills by learning from other chefs—and you will also get a decent income from your participation. Gradually, you will grow your income till you can afford your own place.

CONCLUSION

"When you can't find a job, make one."

Here, we have the entrepreneurial spirit. It's one that is a gamble, but generally the bigger the gamble... the bigger the potential payoff. What we see here is an ideal situation for the convicted felon – he is his own boss and employer. Self-employment pay-offs are substantially larger and provide an easy avenue for "unreported income."

The vast majority of self-employment transactions are in cash or other forms of non-traceable income. Self-employed services are generally found at a substantially lower cost to the consumer, reducing competition and gaining a much wider customer base. It's not uncommon for a self-employed convicted felon to annually make in excess of $50k to $100k, and successfully evade reporting every cent of this income.

In the mindset of the convicted felon, many believe the local, state, and/or federal governments have no right to their personal income, and underreporting their income is a form of retribution or payback for what the criminal system has done to their personal identity and inability to gain traditional employment. Many self-employed ex-felons and non-felons alike believe that what the government doesn't know won't hurt them. The best way to guarantee you are not breaking any tax laws, of course, would be to hire a financial advisor or tax advocate to ensure that the income you do report is in line with all of the government tax laws and liabilities.

In conclusion, if you happen to be an ex-con who is having difficulties in finding and sustaining gainful employment, starting your own business may just be the ideal choice for you. When you take the step to invest in yourself, you just might find yourself making more money than you would working for someone else.

More Titles from Michael Lewiston

Clean Slate: 9 Secrets to Getting a Job, Even With a Felony

Your Ultimate Year of Success: 365 Secret Ways To Be A Better Leader, Get Ahead in Business, and Conquer Your World